The Extranjeros

THE EXTRANJEROS

Selected Documents From the Mexican Side of The Santa Fe Trail 1825-1828

Edited and translated by
DAVID J. WEBER
San Diego State College

STAGECOACH PRESS, SANTA FE

Stagecoach Press, Box 921, Santa Fe, N.M., 87501

INTRODUCTION

THE SANTA FE TRAIL and the exploits of trappers and traders in the Southwestern United States have not suffered from lack of publicity. Journalists, novelists, and historians have told and retold the tales of privation and hardship suffered by the dauntless Missouri merchants who ventured across the Great American Desert risking death by starvation, thirst, and Indian attack to find their way to Mexico or to the Mountains and to claim their reward in silver, mules, or beaver skins.[1] Based largely on material in English, few of these studies have utilized sources from the Mexican side of the Santa Fe Trail.[2] A chief Mexican source, and one that has been much neglected, is the Mexican Archive of New Mexico, housed in the State Records Center and Archives in Santa Fe (hereinafter cited as MANM). The reluctance of researchers to use these documents is understandable in view of the problems of paleography, ungrammatical Spanish, lack of suitable indexing, and the fragmentary nature of the collection during this period. But until these and other Mexican archival sources are more fully exploited, a balanced picture of the activities of Anglo-Americans on Mexico's far northern frontier will not emerge.

The documents included herein are reports of Mexican officials in Taos and Santa Fe, selected for their value in providing a roster of *extranjeros*, or foreigners, in New Mexico during the first years of Mexican administration. Other documents concerning foreigners were also available, but were usually of a more specific nature, dealing with the activities of only a few men. Their inclusion in a small volume of this type could not be justified.

Two of the items included are account books from the custom house at Santa Fe. They usually note the date of arrival of a trader and the amount of duty he paid. In some cases, and these are noted,

[1] The still-sketchy story of the fur trade in the Southwest is best told in Robert Glass Cleland, *This Reckless Breed of Men* (New York, 1950), and J. W. Smurr in the concluding chapters of *The Fur Trade*, 2 vols. (Norman, 1961).

[2] A notable exception is Max L. Moorhead, *New Mexico's Royal Road* (Norman, 1958).

a copy of the trader's *factura*,[3] or trade invoice, also appears. These have not been reproduced in the present volume because they are highly repetitious, lengthy, and seem of little consequence. Two lists of persons who were granted *guías*,[4] or trade permits, to proceed down the Chihuahua Trail from Santa Fe, and three documents listing *extranjeros* in the area are also included.

That this volume begins with 1825 instead of 1821, the date of the effective opening of the Santa Fe Trail, is a matter of necessity rather than one of choice, for documents that concern themselves with Americans are almost non-existent in MANM during the early years of the trade. Custom house records, such as those here published, were probably not kept since Americans were welcomed with such enthusiasm that duties were apparently not collected. In April of 1822, for example, the provincial deputation of New Mexico decided that Americans would have a status equal to that of Mexican citizens.[5] A duty on cotton was to have been collected in 1823 but may have been waived in New Mexico, for Alphonso Wetmore,[6] writing in August, 1824, commented that "when they [the Americans] reach their market, no duties are exacted by the government of the country." In 1824, this rosy picture changed. The men who traveled the road to Santa Fe were obliged to pay a 25 per cent duty on their merchandise.[7] Custom records from this year, however, remain undiscovered.

Although the documents which follow are little more than lists of names, the names in themselves are of particular importance. As Howard Roberts Lamar recently suggested, the conquest of New

[3] The *factura* or *manifiesto*, is discussed by Moorhead in *New Mexico's Royal Road*, pp. 124-25. Moorhead provides a list of representative articles imported by the Santa Fe merchant, on p. 81.

[4] For a discussion of the *guía* see Moorhead, *Royal Road*, p. 139.

[5] Lansing B. Bloom, "New Mexico Under Mexican Administration, 1821-1846," *Old Santa Fe*, I, 2 (October, 1913), 152.

[6] Alphonso Wetmore to Hon. John Scott, Franklin, Mo., August 19, 1824, Senate Document 79, 18th Congress, 1st Session, Serial 116, published in *Santa Fe Trail First Reports: 1825* (Houston, Stagecoach Press, 1960), pp 59-60. Moorhead mentions the 1823 duty in *New Mexico's Royal Road*, p. 125. See also William Albert Bork, *Nuevos aspectos del comercio entre Nuevo Mexico y Misuri 1822-1846* (Mexico, 1944), p. 41, for a discussion of the establishment of the custom house at Santa Fe.

[7] See letter to Messrs. M'Clure and Marmaduke, from Santiago Smith Wilcocks, Feb. 1, 1825, in (Franklin) *Missouri Intelligencer*, August 26, 1825.

Mexico was "A Conquest by Merchants."[8] Yet, these merchants who served as an advance guard for America's manifest destiny have remained largely unknown. True, we know who the star performers were. Such well-known men as Carlos Beaubien, James Ohio Pattie, Antoine Robidoux, Augustus Storrs, David Waldo, Alphonso Wetmore, William Workman, and Ewing Young, appear even within these pages. But if we are to learn more about these trappers and traders—Where did they come from? What motivated them? What were their attitudes toward the trade and toward Mexico?—we must begin by learning more of their names. If we are now able to identify the star performers in this commerce of the prairies, these documents will go a long way toward identifying the rest of the cast.

These lists should be particularly useful in establishing where a trader or trapper was at a specific time. For example, in a recent sketch of Moses Carson it is speculated that "he is reported to have been in Santa Fe as early as 1826."[9] The book of guías granted in 1826-28, item number five, shows clearly that this "report" was true. Moses Carson was in Santa Fe in 1826. To cite another example, James Ohio Pattie is often and rightly accused of confusing the chronology in his well-known Narrative. On at least one occasion, however, Pattie was quite precise. He reported receiving a guía, or trade permit, in the name of his father, Sylvester Pattie, to go in the direction of Chihuahua and Sonora, on September 22, 1827. The book containing guías granted in 1826-1828 shows that Sylvester Pattie did receive a guía on that precise date. It further shows that James O. Pattie had registered the goods of James Glenn, a prominent Santa Fe trader, some three days before his father received a guía.[10]

---

[8] The Far Southwest, 1846-1912 (New Haven, 1966), chapter III.

[9] Harvey L. Carter, "Moses Carson," in The Mountain Men and the Fur Trade of the Far West, LeRoy R. Hafen, ed., vol. II (Glendale, 1965), p. 76. Carter gives no source for this report.

[10] This seems particularly significant in view of Dale Morgan's discovery that the date of Pattie's reported arrival in New Mexico is one entire year too early. See Dale L. Morgan, ed., The West of William H. Ashley (Denver, 1964), p. 306, n. 337. William Goetzmann, in the introduction to the recent Lippincott edition of The Personal Narrative of James O. Pattie (New York, 1962), p. viii, says: "In September of 1827 (Pattie's dates are for the most part inaccurate), ... the Patties made one last hunt into the West...." The guía referred to above appears on p. 121 of this edition with a date of 1829—a printer's error if one compares it with the original edition which says 1827.

The following items appear in chronological order, each being preceded by a brief description of its contents. Four documents are from MANM, two are from the Ritch Papers at The Huntington Library, San Marino, California, and one document from the Archivo General de la Secretaría de la Relaciones Exteriores, Mexico City. Original orthography has been preserved throughout. More often than not, accents are missing in the original document. They remain missing in these transcriptions. Correct names have occasionally been supplied in the customary square brackets, but the more obvious errors are scarcely in need of editorial comment. Because the handwriting of these officials is something less than clear, the researcher who believes that I have made an error may well be correct and is urged to consult the original. In cases where I have relied on intuition, however, a question mark appears beside the name. Notes and introductory comments are designed to clarify the documents; to attempt to comment upon individuals would be an endless task.

Should this volume achieve any degree of utility, the credit must go to Dr. Myra Ellen Jenkins, Senior Archivist at the State Records Center of New Mexico, who gave me my first lessons in paleography of the Mexican period, and to Dr. Donald Cutter of the University of New Mexico, who aroused my interest and has directed my research in this area.

DAVID J. WEBER

San Diego State College
San Diego, California
September, 1967

CONTENTS

Document   *Page*

1   Custom House Records, Santa Fe, 1825 15

2   Report on Foreigners, Antonio Narbona, Santa Fe,
    February 1, 1826 19

3   Miscellaneous *Guías*, 1825 23

4   Treasury Report, Santa Fe, 1826-1827 25

5   Book of *Guías*, Santa Fe, 1826-1828 29

6   Report on Departures of Foreigners, Manuel Martínez,
    Taos, April 7, 1827 35

7   Reports on Arrivals of Foreigners: 39
    A. Santa Fe, July, 1827.
    B. Taos, November, 1827

The Extranjeros

I

Custom House Records
Santa Fe / 1825

⚑ *Book which consists of exact copies of accounts granted to the foreigners of North America who have introduced merchandise subject to the payment of fifteen per cent importation duty and three per cent excise tax* [derecho de consumo], *in the present year of 1825. In the National Custom House of the Territory of New Mexico.*

Ritch Papers, No. 81, reproduced by permission of The Huntington Library, San Marino, California.

Editor's Comment

HIS DOCUMENT is unique in that it includes copies, in Spanish, of *facturas*, their dates, and the places at which they were drawn up. Each entry reads something like this:

> William Workman, citizen of the United States of North America, has presented in this National Custom House of New Mexico an original trade invoice from Franklin, with the date of April 25 of the present year, which contains four *tercios* with the following goods:

A list of the merchandise then follows. Its total value and import duty are indicated.

A surprising number of traders straggled into Santa Fe before the arrival of the main caravan in July. Those who checked into the custom house between July 7 and July 15 were probably of the large party that rendezvoused near Fort Osage in mid-May. This caravan reportedly consisted of one hundred and five men, although only forty-seven are recorded as arriving in Santa Fe before July 15th. Some discrepancy is understandable for many members of the caravan did not possess merchandise, but were in the employ of others. Some may have paid their duty at Taos or San Miguel, and others not at all. Not recorded as arriving in Santa Fe, for example, were caravan leaders "Thompson, Stanley, Emmons, 'Night and Shackelford," as well as the captain, Augustus Storrs.[11]

This was not the only party to set out for New Mexico in the spring of 1825. On June 18th, the *Missouri Intelligencer* noted that "already has a large party left Tennessee, and another from Alabama." Perhaps the men with *facturas* from Nashville, Jackson (Tennessee) and Huntsville (Alabama), cited in this document, were from these parties. The majority, however, were Missourians: Franklin, Columbia, Boon and a Jackson and a Nashville also being in that state. Later that fall parties under the leadership of Sylvestre S. Pratte, Antoine Robidoux and George C. Sibley also reached New Mexico Evidence of their presence appears in subsequent documents.

---

11 Letter from Camp near Fort Osage, May 16, 1825, in the (Franklin) *Missouri Intelligencer*, June 4, 1825.

March 27	James Dempsy	
March 29	Gratios [?] Geaibu [Geaboux?]	
March 30	John Longhhir	
April 3	William Rennicke and company	Lexxington and Franklin (Mo.), Nov. 2 & Oct. 29, 1824.
April 11	Ewing Young	
April 20	Wm Anderson	
April 27	Richard Campbell y May?	
April 27	Paul Baillio	
n. d.	M. S. Cerré	
May 18	Thomas H. Boggs	
June 3	James Dempsey	
July 7	John Kenkeade	Franklin and Colombia, April 25, and May 2.
July 8	Alexander Calvin	Colombia, April 17 & 25.
July 8	William Workman	Franklin, April 25.
July 8	Samuel Gawesan	Colombia April 27.
July 8	Robert Griffith	Colombia, April 27.
July 8	Nicholas Gentry	two *facturas,* Colombia, April 28
July 8	George Bartley	Boon, April 17.
July 8	John Remison	Franklin, April 30.
July 8	Jeoquin R. Marble	Lexington, May 14.
July 8	Welliam Lee Weine	Colombia, n. d.
July 8	Amos Barnes	Colombia, n. d.
July 9	Fébeanes[?] Carel	Colombia, April 26.
July 9	James Sullenger	Franklin, April 25.
July 8	George Munro	Franklin, April 25.
July 9	Stephan Mury[?]	Colombia, April 25.
July 9	Louis Snitzler[?]	Franklin, April 30.
July 9	George Wallit	Franklin, April 25
July 9	Daniel Curey	Franklin, April 21
July 9	John Nichols	Franklin, April 26
July 9	William Yearhusse[?] [Gearhart?]	no location, April 28 & 29.
July 9	Mathew Thinkead [Kinkead]	

[17]

July 10	Isaac Gearhart	factura was "drowned" in a river.
July 13	Sam Ghabs	Nashville, Feb. 19
July 13	Wm. R. Seatt	Colombia, March 8
July 13	S m Voorhees	Chalotte, April 13
July 14	John H. Meney	2 facturas, Madison, March 3
July 14	Andrew Nesbitt	Charlotte, March 26
July 14	Alfred R. Stevery and Wilson	2 facturas Jackson, April 17
July 14	H. B. Fleillere[?]	Nashville, March 2
July 14	Wm. H. Bitty	Carlota, March 15
July 14	Bird. Thos L.[?] Smith	Nashville, March 18
July 14	———? Embrey	Jackson, March 31
July 14	William Braden	Nashville, Feb. 15
July 14	——uson A. Hurt and company	Huntiville, March 8
July 14	James Caezhan[?]	Huntreville, March 9
July 14	[?]	
July 14	Absalom Molsic[?]	no location, March 30
July 14	Isaac Estell	no location, March 2
July 15	Benj. Smith	Jackson, March 18
July 15	James Key	Jackson, March 12
July 15	Payton Sullivan	Jackson, March 17
July 15	John Chickering	no location, March 15
July 15	Joseph Royal	Jackson, April 2
July 15	John A. Townsend	2 facturas, March 18 & 19
July 15	Daniel Leffefraw [Lefebre?]	Colombia, March 14
n. d.	Robert W. Morris	name appears on a blank page

2

Report on Foreigners
Antonio Narbona
Santa Fe / February 1 / 1826

TERRITORY OF NEW MEXICO
🖾 *Report which shows the foreigners who have arrived here from the United States of North America, with the declaration of their names, districts where they reside, business in which they engage themselves, and passports which they have presented.*

Archivo General de la
Secretaría de Relaciones
Exteriores, Mexico City.

Editor's Comment

WRITTEN by Governor Antonio Narbona, this report was probably his first response to a circular of November 19, 1825, which ordered each Mexican state and territory to make a monthly report of the number and movements of all foreigners to the Secretaría de Relaciones Interiores y Exteriores. It does not pretend to list all arrivals, but only those who remained in New Mexico. The first sixteen names on Narbona's list, from Armstrong to Roberto, settled at Santa Fe, while the remainder made their homes at Taos.

names	business	Passports with which they have emigrated
Brazo fuerte [Armstrong]	hunter	without passport
Eliseo [Elisha Stanley?]	merchant	without passport
Escoto [?]	silversmith	without passport
Juan	carpenter	without passport
Jorge Chibley [Sibley]	Commissioned for the cleaning of roads	Only presented a letter and plan of his commission which has been sent to the Supreme Government.
Abrahan [Abram]	Servant of the Commissioner [negro]	
Jose Brone [Brown]	accompanied the commissioner	
Tomas	iron smith	without passport
Juan Worde [Ward]	merchant	without passport
Francisco Similiano	interpreter	without passport
Julian [William] Anderson	merchant	with passport from his government
Gentry Fuyd [Floyd]	merchant	without passport
Jorge W. West	cabinet maker	without passport
Diego Santiago	hat maker	without passport
Juan	painter	without passport
Roberto	tinsmith	without passport
Francisco Lackleer	merchant	With passport from the governor of St. Louis
Pedro Connoles [Connelley?]	merchant	With passport from the military commander of the Fort
Julian Gass	merchant	Without passport
Faxbe Nolan with two servants	merchant	With passport from the Military Commander of the Fort [Fort Atkinson?]

[21]

names	business	Passports with which they have emigrated
Matias Guingueer [?]	merchant	Without passport
Guillermo	merchant	Without passport
Juan Roles	Without occupation	With passport from the Government of St. Louis
Juan Cristobal Loba	Without occupation	Without passport
Miguel Axrono [?]	Without occupation	Without passport
Luis Gruero [?]	servant	
Bautista Sanserman [Baptiste St. Germain]	servant	
Lamaris [Luis Lamoré]	servant	
Anastasio Cariel	servant	
Francisco Rubidu [Robidoux]	merchant	Without passport
Miguel Rubidu	merchant	Without passport
Antonio Rubidu	merchant	Without passport

🍃 *Explanation*

The individuals mentioned in this report remain in this Terítory as transients without demonstrating, up to now, an intention of settling themselves. Nevertheless, the merchants, in order to sell their goods, they remain for some time in the towns where they employ themselves, preferring among these Taos and the capital of Santa Fe, where [in Santa Fe] the silversmith, carpenter, ironsmith, cabinet maker, hat maker, painter, and tinsmith have located their workshops.

In the aforementioned port of Taos, which is the frontier, there commonly reside a greater number of foreigners. By it being the edge of our populated area, it affords a refuge which many take advantage of without giving knowledge of their presence.

The Americans Colmoore, John Gregg, Tomas Abeciaon[?], Luis Rubidu, and Francisco Siore are not included in this report because they have passed to the states of Chihuahua and Sonora. Augustus Storrs, named consul by his government, is not included, because he is to be found in El Paso del Norte,

Santa Fe 10 de Febrero de 1826

Antonio Narbona

3

Miscellaneous Guias / 1825

Mexican Archives of
New Mexico.

Editor's Comment

THE FIRST *guías* in the Mexican Archives of New Mexico appear in the year 1825.[12] *Guías* 8 through 12 appear together, but the remainder are scattered throughout the documents of that year. At least 26 *guías* were granted in 1825, but only 12 remain. An invoice of merchandise, or *factura*, accompanied each *guía*.

July 20	#8	J. McVoorhees	
July 20	#9	Wm. R. Scott	
July 21	#10	L. Weton	
July 25	#12	Jhon Townsem [John Townsend?]	
July 25	#13	Benjamin Smith	
July 25	#14	Joseph Hodsodon [Hudson?]	
August 9		Kinuardo Ballinger	(Factura only)
August 22	#17	James Parke	
August 22	#16	Edward Beaven [r?]	to Sonora
Sept. 23		Richard Campbell ⎱	⎰ Requests, #13 &
Sept. 23		Ira A. Emmons ⎰	⎱ #10, for *guías* to Sonora
October 30	#26	John E. Parrish	to Sonora & Chihuahua

---

[12] Specific rules for the issuance of *guías* were not formulated until the fall of 1824 (Circular, Secretaría de Hacienda, October 27, 1824, in Official Decrees and Circulars, Box 4 [1824], MANM).

4

Treasury Report
Santa Fe / 1826-1827

Account which shows the transfer of the funds of the Public Treasury of the Federation, which Don Juan Bautista Vigil made to me [Agustín Durán], *by virtue of the agreement of the Most Excellent Provincial Deputation of this Territory. On January 12, 1826, the Political and Military Governor of this same territory, Colonel Don Antonio Narbona, ordered that I should receive these funds provisionally, during the suspension that the aforementioned body has decided to impose on the said Don Juan Bautista Vigil. This individual has made the aforementioned transfer to me in the following terms:*

New Mexico, 1826.
Mexican Archives of

Editor's Comment

HE "account" which follows this elaborate title proceeds to list income and expenditures of the public treasury from January of 1826 to the end of January of 1827. Included among the incoming funds are duties received from the traders listed herein. *Factura* numbers are given, but the *facturas* themselves were not copied into this "account." American names first appear in August. It should be noted that a number of the names which appear in January of 1827, also appeared at an earlier date. Tomás South, for example, is listed as arriving in both December and January. Since it would have been impossible for him to cross the Trail twice in a month's time, it may be assumed that on one of these occasions South's *factura* was entered into the "account" and South need not have been present. Thus, the presence of a trader's *factura* in this document does not necessarily indicate the physical presence of the trader.

Among the funds which Agustín Durán received from his predecessor were duties paid by several Americans: Sylvestre Pratte, "the four Americans Robidour [Robidoux]," "Kinker [possibly James Kirker]," Benjamin "Smitt," and William Anderson. These men had probably arrived in the fall of 1825.

AUGUST 1826

Factura

#		
#1	Nathaniel Syms	August 1, 1826
#2	William Hersen	Aug. 1
#3	Thos.[?] B. Smith	Aug. 1
#4	Elias Mead	Aug. 3
#5	William Gayharte	Aug. 10
#6	Thomas Barnes	Aug. 10
#7	Sammuel Lamme (signature)	Aug. 11
#8	Mical Luisbzlez(?)	Aug. 11
#9	Richard D. Shakelford	Aug. 11
#10	C Enteand[?]	Aug. 18

SEPTEMBER 1826

#11	Presvitt Folesy	factura d. Aug. 29

#12 Moses B. Carson
#13 Michel Suelsler [Suisla, according to another copy of this document]
#14 Rugh [Hugh?] Green and company
#15 Isaac Wright
#16 Francisco Samuel
#17 Ewing Young
#18 James Dempse
#19 Eliseo Stanley (signature)

Listed among the outgoing funds of this month is a payment to Santiago Dauglass[?] and Jorge Westt which represents the return of a deposit paid at Chihuahua.

OCTOBER

no Americans

NOVEMBER

#20 Silbestre Pratte
#21 Pablo Baillio [signature]

DECEMBER

#22 Tomás Boggs
#23 James L. Dobbin
#24 John Means
#25 William Workman

[27]

DECEMBER

Factura
#26 Samuel M.Clurz [McClure]
#27 Thomás Konr [Connor?]
#28 Uurl [Earl?] asjon and company
#29 Ricardo y Tomás South
#30 Elosege Ja Neson[?] [Elisha
      Johnson]

Listed among the outgoing funds of this month is a payment to Jorge
Westt and Antonio Rovidour which represents the return of a deposit
paid at El Paso.

JANUARY 1827

Pablo Baillio
Ewing Yaung [Young]
Tomás Boggs
Samuel Lamme [signature]
William Gayehart
Moses Michil
Moses Michel
James Dempse

Chas Pentalsa [?]
Eliseo Estanley [signature]
Jhon Means
Moses B. Carsón
Michel Suisla
Thomas South
Ellrage [Eldridge?] Jackson

5

Book of Guias
Santa Fe / 1826-1828

🖝 *Book which contains* guías *granted by this administration in the years of 1826 and 1827 [and 1828].*

Custom House of the frontier of Santa Fe in the Territory of New Mexico.

Mexican Archives of
New Mexico, 1826.

Editor's Comment

THE *GUÍAS* copied in this book contain, in most cases, the destination of the merchant, the business he was involved in, the date the *guía* was issued, and the date by which he was expected to return. With the exception of those noted, all were going to Chihuahua and Sonora. The recipients of these *guías* did not necessarily accompany their goods, although this appears to have been the usual case. When the owner of the merchandise was not going along, the name of the clerk entrusted with the goods was sometimes indicated, as in the case of *guía* no. 40 which reads, "Santiago Glen con Santiago O. Patis." James Glenn also received *guía* no. 42, "con José M.ª Baca." Obviously, he did not travel with either of these men because he was still around a month later to receive *guía* no. 47. On this occasion he probably headed down the trail to Chihuahua.

Guía no. 1 in this book was not the first to be issued in 1826. Gentry Floyd, a prominent trader, received *guía* no. 3 from Santa Fe on February 27,[13] almost three months before the first *guía* appears in this book.

Requests for *guías* from 1826 through 1828 appear at random in MANM. Except for the *facturas* which accompany them, these add little information to this "book" and are not, therefore, reproduced. Several are of importance, however, and are mentioned in the notes that accompany this document.

---

[13] A copy of this *guía* appears in the Documentos de la Ciudad de Juárez (Microfilm at University of Texas at El Paso, Reel 34, 1826, I, p. 114).

Guía

#1	Luis Robidux con Manuel Martin	May 19 (El Paso)
#2	Elias Meas	n. d.
#3	Eliseo Stanley	August 29
#4	Samuel P. Lamme	August 28
#5	William Green	n. d. (no destination given)
#6	Eliseo Stanley[14]	[August 30]
#7	B YBos[?] Meas	September 2
#8	Paul Anderson	n. d.
#9	Gorge Weste	n. d.
#10	Ramon Garcia	n. d. (El Paso and Sonora)
#11	Paul Anderson	n. d.
#12	Samuel M. Clur [McClur]	n. d.
#13	John G. Parritt	n. d.
#14	Santiago Pursel [Purcell]	n. d.
#15	James G. Sreaneny[?] [Sweeney?]	n. d.
#16	Frances S. Samuel	n. d.
#17	Gorge Weste[15]	September 17
#18	Eliseo Stanley	n. d.
#19	William Anderson	n.d. (Chihuahua)
#20	Samuel P. Lamme	n. d.
#21	Houck & Ynby [Inby?]	October 14
#22	Antonio Robidour [Robidoux]	n. d. (no destination given)
#23	Carlos Boubin [Beaubien]	November 21
#24	Samuel Lamme	November 22
#25	M. Carson[16]	December 8

[14] Stanley's request for a *guía* appears in the Ritch Papers, no. 64, dated August 30, 1826. Hugh Stephenson also signed the request, which was granted as *guía* no. 6 and, acting as clerk for Stanley, apparently took the merchandise south. Stanley apparently followed his clerk with more merchandise in September (see *guía* no. 18).

[15] The name of George Weste on this *guía* could be an error. A request for a *guía* appears in MANM, dated Sept. 17 and signed by George Armstrong, was granted as *guía* no. 17.

[16] Moses Carson was probably accompanied by his brother, William. A request for a *guía* appears in MANM, dated December 8 and signed by "Wm. Carson & Co." It was granted as *guía* no. 25.

Guía

#26	[missing]	
#27	Elbridge [Jackson]	[April 7][17]
#28	Santiago Posel [Purcell?]	July 13,
#29	[Amos Marney]	[July 14][18]
#30	Lic.o [Licenciado] Manuel Escudero with José Agustin de Escudero	July 1
#31	Johnhun[?] Fletcher	July 28
#32	Munion[?]	July 28
#33	Eenhree [Henry?] S. Mahany [Mahoney?]	August 2
#34	Alan Withers	August 2
#35	Michael Eley	August 3
#36	J. Johnson	August 6
#37	B[?] H. Harison with Paul Anderson	August 7
#38	Ricjar Stows with William Green	August 12
#39	John Pierson with George W. West	August 12
#40	Santiago Glén with Santiago O. Patis [Pattie]	August 19
#41	Vizente Provencio	August 28
#42	James Glenn with José M.a Baca	September 19
#43	Jacob Jones	September 20
#44	Silvestre Pattie	September 22
#45	Gentri Floyd	October 3
#46	Michael Eléy	October 1
#47	Santiago Glenn	October 20
#48	John C. Henley[?]	October 21
#49	Ricardo Storrs with Augustus Storrs	October 21
#50	Felipe Tramel	December 14

[17] There is no record of *guía* no. 27 in the "Cuaderno," but a request for a *guía* signed by Elbridge Jackson and dated April 7, 1827, appears in MANM. This request is numbered as *guía* no. 27. The merchandise was apparently taken south by Jackson's clerk, William Green. Written in English at the bottom of the request is "I sign the within bill to Paul Anderson May 5th 1827," signed Elbridge Jackson.

[18] A request for a *guía* dated July 14, 1827, appears in MANM. Signed by one Amos Marney and dated "Colonvia [Columbia, Missouri]," May 4, 1827, it is accompanied by a *factura*. It seems reasonable to suppose that Marney was the recipient of the missing *guía* no. 29.

Guía

#51   Luis de Fies with Samuel Chambres   December 20
      [Chambers]
#52   Luis de Fies   December 20

                    1828

#53   Pablo Baillio with Manuel Alvarez   January 22
#54   Felipe Tomson and Juan Person   March 28
      [Pierson] with the former.
#55   Waller with Jacobo Jones   July 19
                                              (Chihuahua)
#56   Juan Loughlin with Pablo Anderson   July 19
#57   Pablo Anderson with Juan Loklin   n. d.
      [Loughlin?]
#58   Joaquin Esques [?] with Francisco   July 22 (Sonora)
      Romo
#59   Santiago Prosel [Purcell?]   July 23 (Sonora)
#60   Santiago Posel [Purcell?]   July 23 (Sonora)

#1   M———[?] Lanpson[?]   July 28
#2   Thefisos[?] Porter with [H]ammund   July 2[?]
#3   Jose Resnolds [Reynolds]   August 14
#4   Sbroleher [Strother] Rennick   August 14
#5   Salomon Gane[?]   August 19
#6   Gentrey Floyd with Jose Washington   August 22
      Knox
#7   Alfonso Wtmore [Wetmore] with   August 22
      Henrique Connully   (Chihuahua)
#8   Juan Hardeman   August 22
#9   Carson and Boon   August 22
                                              (Chihuahua)
#10   Santiago Glenn with Alfonso   August 22
      Wetmore   (Chihuahua)
#11   James K. Cason with Wllian Thomas   August 22
#12   Vicente Provencio   August 22 (Sonora)
#13   Agusto Storrs   August 22
#14   Juan Ant.o Baca with Jesus Baca   n. d.
#15   Visente Otero with Jose Antonio   September 1
      Otero

Guía

#16	David Wolda [Waldo]	September 2
#17	Vizente Armijo	n. d.
#18	Patricio Ryder	September 3
#19	Patricio Huslo[?]	September 3
#20	Enriquez y Foley [Henry E. Foley or Henry and Foley?]	September 3
#21	J. Belcher	August 29
#22	Tomas Scott with Juan C. Fibley[?]	September 6
#23	Jorge Brasofuerte [George Armstrong]	September 11
#24	Juan L. Pateron [Paterson]	September 11
#25	Santiago Glen with Juan Jonson	September 21
#26	Santiago Glen with Juan Jonson	September 21
#27	Guillermo Hieth [Heath?]	September 25

6

Report on Departures of Foreigners.
Manuel Martínez
Taos / April 7 / 1827

✎ *Report which provides information regard-
ing the foreigners who have been in this jurisdiction of Taos, and have left on a journey
from the month of January of this year up to
the present date.*

Mexican Archives of
New Mexico, 1827.

Editor's Comment

𝕋HIS REPORT, by Alcalde Manuel Martínez, provides an interesting picture of three groups of foreigners which left Taos —that most foreign of New Mexican towns—during the early months of 1827. The first group, composed of Missouri merchants returning home, set out from Taos on April 6. By July, at least six of these traders were making plans to return to New Mexico. José T. Boggs, Paul Baillio, John Tharp, Manuel Alvarez, Gervais Nolan and Louis Robidoux were part of a larger group of thirty-three that received a permit on July 23, from William Clark, Superintendent of Indian Affairs, to pass through Indian country to the "Province of Mexico."[19] Also included in this group were Michael S. Cerré, Vicente Guion, Francis Guerin, and Lewis Howard, the remainder being Mexicans. A number of these foreigners showed up again in Taos in November, according to the Martínez report which follows.

The groups led by Francisco Robidoux and Sylvestre S. Pratte, which Martinez also identifies in this document, were almost certainly trapping parties. This report contains two of the most complete known lists of trappers involved in the elusive Southwestern fur trade. It reveals a surprising number of persons of French ancestry operating out of Taos. Many of these will be familiar to the specialist.

---

[19] Ritch Papers, no. 95. This permit is reproduced in facsimile in Robert Glass Cleland, *This Reckless Breed of Men* (New York, 1950), facing p. 202.

In the party which left on the sixth day of the current month, destined for the Missouri, are the following:

Jose Tomas Boggs

Paul Baillio

Pohn [John] Tharp

William Anderson

Richare L. Sontt [South?]

Thomas Soutt [South?]

Samuel Nelson

Samuel D. Lamma[?]

Alvin Reed

Jean Lusyan[?]

Samuel Perry

Francis Samuel

Pohn [John] Brown

Jean Pierre

Louis Dethiers

Louis Roubidoux

Jervain Nollán

Francis Broun

Manuel de Alvarez

———◆◆◆———

In a party which left in the month of January of the present [year], whose date I am unable to remember, and the said party is that of Silvestre Pratte whose destination is outside the boundaries of the Mexican Federations, are the following:

Manuel Lefaivre

S. Desporte

F. Braie

G. Olivier

Pled Riche

Sénecal

Luis Ambroise

Bautista Chauno

Jn Vaillant

Duchaine

Vertefeville

Vertefeville fils

Livernois

S.t Vrain

Laforest

Beaubien

Lafargue

Glas

Broun [Brown]

S.t Germain

Simon Clert

Jurome

———◆◆◆———

In another party which left in the month of March of the present [year], whose date I am unable to remember, and the said party is that of Francisco Roubidou, whose destination is to go to retrieve some caches in the direction of the land of the Utes, are the following:

Dionicio Julian
   [Denis Julien]
Bautista Trudean [Trudeau]
Jose Neuture
Man.l Gervais
Ant.o Blanchare
Ant.o Leroux
Bautista Chalifon
   [Charlefoux]

Pablo Loise
Mauricio Ledue
   [Maurice LeDuc]
Francisco Gervais
Metote
Charles Chonteau
Jules Declovette

All of these are those who have left, as is noted above, and attesting to its correctness I sign this report today, April 7, 1827.

Manuel Martinez

7

Reports on Arrivals
of Foreigners

———◆◆◆———

Santa Fe / July / 1827

Territory of New Mexico
✎ *Report of the foreigners who have arrived in the Territory in the month of July, 1827, in compliance with the circular of November 19, 1825, transmitted by the Secretaría de Relaciones.*

———◆◆◆———

Taos / November / 1827

Territory of New Mexico
✎ *Report of the foreigners who have arrived in the Territory in the month of November, 1827, in compliance with the circular of November 19, 1825, transmitted by the Secretaría de Relaciones.*

Ritch Papers, No. 96, reproduced by permission of The Huntington Library, San Marino, California.

Editor's Comment

THE TWO DOCUMENTS which follow appear on printed forms. That of July is from Santa Fe and that of November, from Taos. In addition to the name, country, profession and place where the foreigner intended to settle, the forms have spaces to indicate the source of the foreigner's passport, its date, and its number. These spaces were left blank on both documents. The form also asks for the place from which the foreigner traveled and the date on which he presented himself in Mexico. The first document indicates that all left from Missouri and arrived in Santa Fe on July 8, while the second document reveals varying points of departure. All reportedly arrived on November 12.

Most, if not all of those who checked into the custom house at Santa Fe in July of 1827 were from the large caravan that assembled on the Santa Fe Trail in mid-May. Reported to contain some 105 men, this company was thought to be "the largest which has traversed this route." Among the officers and leaders were Ezekiel Williams, Presley Samuel, James Glenn, James L. Collins, Richard Gentry, Joseph Reynolds, Joshua Fletcher, John Dade, James Ramsay, S. Turley, J. Rennison, R. Stowers, L. Morrison, A. Barnes, and D. Workman. [20] With the exception of Williams, Turley and Workman, all of these men are represented in the following document. John Pearson, from England, who gave his occupation as preacher upon arriving at Santa Fe, was Chaplain of the caravan. "A gentleman of very agreeable manners and of very handsome scientific and theological attainments," according to Augustus Storrs, the Reverend Mr. Pearson may be the first professed Protestant minister to enter Santa Fe.

---

[20] Letter from Augustus Storrs, Santa Fe Trace, 120 miles west of Franklin, May 18, 1827, in the (Fayette) *Missouri Intelligencer*, May 24, 1827.

Territory of New Mexico

Report of the foreigners who have arrived in the territory in the month of July, 1827, in compliance with the circular of November 19, 1825, transmitted by the Secretaría de Relaciones.

name	country	profession	place of residence or where they settle
Michael Eley	Virginia	merchant	Santa Fe
Juan Dade	"	"	"
Santiago Ramsay	Kentucky	laborer	"
Ricardo Gentry	"	"	"
Hugh Harrison	"	"	"
Juan Pearson	England	Preacher	"
Juan S. Patton	Kentucky	Carpenter	"
Juan Rennison	England	merchant	"
Amos Marney	Missouri	"	"
Santiago Glen	Kentucky	"	"
Augustus Storrs	Missouri	"	"
Ricardo Stowers	Kentucky	"	"
Joshua Fletcher	N. Hampshire	"	"
Benjamin Harrison	Kentucky	"	"
Luis Morrison	"	"	"
Juan Swan	"	"	"
Nathaniel Syms	"	"	"
Juan Jones	"	"	"
Cristoval Hough	"	"	"
Daniel Munro	"	"	"
Guillermo Taylor	"	"	"
Santiago Collins	"	"	Taos
Felipe Collins	"	"	Rio abajo
Bird Lawless	"	"	"
Carlos Rector	"	"	"
Edwin M. Ryland	Virginia	"	Bado
Santiago Feland	Missouri	"	Rio abajo
Abraham Barnes	"	"	Taos
Guillermo Thomas	"	"	Taos
Pedro Collier	"	"	"
José Reynolds	"	"	Rio abajo

[41]

name	country	profession	place of residence or where they settle
Guillermo Moppin	Missouri	merchant	Rio abajo
Robert Lucky	"	"	"
Presly Samuel	"	"	"
Santiago Dempsey	"	"	"
Benjamin Barnes	"	"	"

NOTES

Eighty-four foreigners from North America arrived in this Territory on the eighth day of the current month. If only thirty-six appear in this report, it is because the Alcaldes of the border towns of Bado [San Miguel del Vado] and Taos, places in the Territory through which the foreigners enter, do not prepare this report in detail as they have been instructed to do. They fear to be disobeyed by the foreigners and do not have the strength to make themselves respected. But this is the first time, during the period of my command, that they have arrived in the Territory. I will see to it in the future, at any risk, that they fill out this report with proper care.

Although all the foreigners are not listed in this report, if I am correct, those that appear in this report, as well as those who are not in it, totally lack passports.

Of the foreigners who have arrived in this Territory, many have remained, and some have married without citizenship papers. I must warn you that the worst of them already know our language. Some do not have employment or means of subsistence. When their countrymen arrive, so that they may give them something, they are the ones who introduce contraband and even induce them to commit shameless acts [groserías] and other offenses of which I have already spoken to the Supreme Government. I ask to be told what to do with such foreigners: if they should remain as they are or if I should demand that they return to their country.

[unsigned]

Territory of New Mexico

Report of the foreigners who have arrived in the Territory in the month of November, 1827, in compliance with the circular of November 19, 1825, transmitted by the Secretaría de Relaciones.

name	country	proceeding from	profession	place of residence or where they settle
Pablo Baillio	St. Louis	St. Louis	merchant	In this territory
Juan Hood	Scotland	Brownsville	merchant	"
Juan Tharp	N. Car.	Fort Osage	servant	"
Santiago Swop	Kentucky	Franklin	servant	"
Juan Brown	"	Lafayette	servant	"
Juan S. Langham	Virginia	Franklin	merchant	"
Mig.l S. Cerré	St. Louis	St. Louis	merchant	"
Basil Paillane[?]	Canada	St. Louis	servant	"
Felipe U. Thompson	Virginia	Franklin	tailor	Taos or Santa Fe
Samuel D. Lucas	Kentucky	Brwnville	merchant	In this territory
Roberto T. Howe	"	"	merchant	"
Felipe Trammell	Virginia	Franklin	merchant	"
Julian Trammell	Kentucky	"	merchant	"
Louis De Ehiers[?]	Liege	St. Louis	doctor	Mexico
Julian Yong [Young]	Tenesee	Lexington	blacksmith (Albeitar)	In this territory
Vicente Guion	St. Louis	St. Louis	merchant	"
Fran.co Guerin	France	St. Louis	merchant	"
Manuel de Alvarez	Leon	St. Louis	merchant	"
Gervasio Nollen	Canada	St. Louis	gunsmith	Taos

The foregoing report comments on, and contains the names of the foreigners who have arrived in this jurisdiction of Taos, the 12th day of the current month, and to certify it, upon sending it to the Political Governor of this Territory, I sign it as the constitutional alcalde, today, November 19, 1827.

Manuel Martinez

A WORD ABOUT THE PRINTING

This limited edition was designed by Jack D. Rittenhouse and printed at his Stagecoach Press in Santa Fe. Body text was set in Linotype Caledonia, with headings handset in Centaur and Hammer American Uncial type. Printed on a hand-operated press, using Carnival paper with a "handmade" finish.